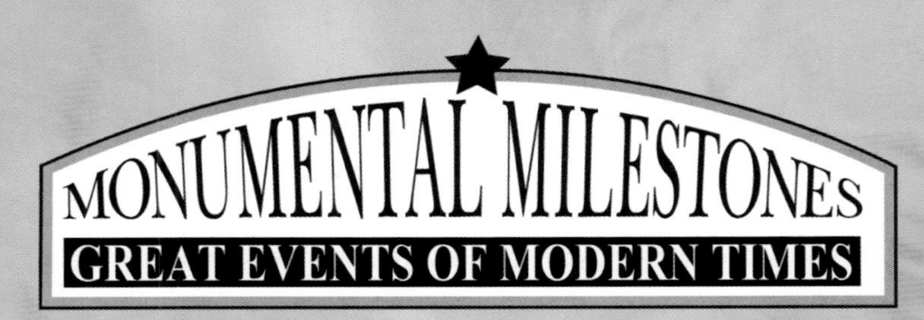

Breaking the Sound Barrier

The Story of Chuck Yeager

General Chuck Yeager took one of the most famous rides in history when he broke the sound barrier in 1947.

Mitchell Lane PUBLISHERS
P.O. Box 196
Hockessin, Delaware 19707

Titles in the Series

The Dawn of Aviation:
The Story of the Wright Brothers

Pearl Harbor and the War with Japan

Breaking the Sound Barrier:
The Story of Chuck Yeager

Top Secret: The Story of the
Manhattan Project

The Story of the Holocaust

The Civil Rights Movement

Exploring the North Pole:
The Story of Robert Edwin
Peary and Matthew Henson

The Story of the Great Depression

The Cuban Missile Crisis:
The Cold War Goes Hot

The Fall of the Berlin Wall

Disaster in the Indian Ocean
Tsunami, 2004

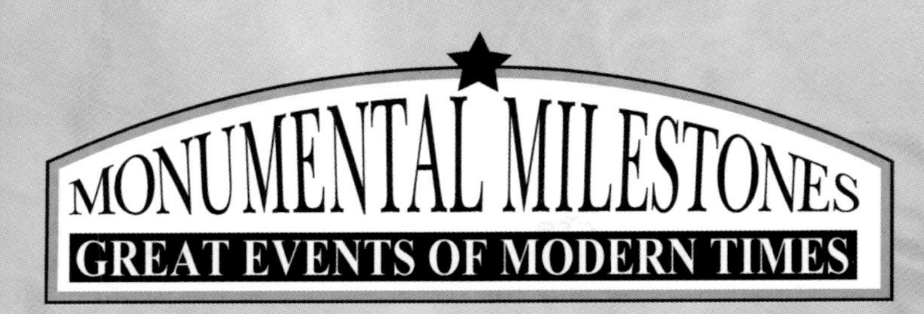

Breaking the Sound Barrier

The Story of Chuck Yeager

General Chuck Yeager's pioneering spirit in the aviation industry helped make him one of America's great heroes.

Susan Sales Harkins

Printing 2 3 4 5 6 7 8 9

Library of Congress Cataloging-in-Publication Data
Harkins, Susan Sales.
Breaking the sound barrier : the story of Chuck Yeager / by Susan Harkins.
p. cm. — (Monumental milestones)
ISBN 1-58415-398-9 (library bound)
1. Yeager, Chuck, 1923—Juvenile literature. 2. Air politics—United States—Biography—Juvenile literature. 3. High-speed aeronautics—History—Juvenile literature. I. Title. II. Series.
TL540.Y4H37 2005
623.74'6048'092—dc22 2004030264

ISBN-13: 9781584153986

ABOUT THE AUTHOR: Susan Sales Harkins has been a full-time writer since 1992. Before that, she taught general computing classes at a local business college. Now, she specializes in computer journalism and children's educational literature. Susan's most recent book is *The New SAT Exam Cram with Sample Tests on CD-ROM*, by Que Publishing. Her favorite pastime is pursuing her grandchildren in rural Kentucky where she lives with a few animals including one of the two-legged variety (her husband).

PHOTO CREDITS: All photos—Official U.S. Air Force photos.

PUBLISHER'S NOTE: This story is based on the author's extensive research, which she believes to be accurate. Documentation of such research is contained on page 47.

The internet sites referenced herein were active as of the publication date. Due to the fleeting nature of some web sites, we cannot guarantee they will all be active when you are reading this book.

PPC4

Contents

Breaking the Sound Barrier
The Story of Chuck Yeager

Susan Sales Harkins

*For Your Information

Chuck Yeager enlisted in the Air Corps as an aircraft mechanic.

As a youth, he wasn't fascinated by airplanes nor did he have any aspirations or secret yearnings to be a pilot. In fact, he got sick the first few times he flew. Eventually, he conquered the sickness and learned to love flying better than anything else.

Riding a Bomb into History

On the morning of October 14, 1947, Captain Chuck Yeager's heart beat faster than usual. Sitting in the cockpit of an experimental aircraft was normal, but today's flight promised to be either spectacular or deadly.

As usual, the X-1 was hanging from the belly of a B-29 bomber that was flying 20,000 feet in the air. All that stood between Chuck and the record books—or death—was a release cable. Soon that cable would pop and the X-1 and its courageous pilot would drop from the mother ship and into the bright morning sky.

While jammed into the X-1's small cockpit with his knees bent up to his chin, Chuck thought about the flight to come. Would he be the first to fly faster than the speed of sound? Or would he scatter to the winds in a million small pieces when he slammed against the invisible wall known as the sound barrier? There was only one way to know for sure.

"Are you ready?" Chuck finally heard through his headset.

He didn't hesitate. He was as ready as he would ever be.

"Yes," was Chuck's simple answer.

The cable popped. Suddenly, Chuck was free falling toward earth—plummeting through open sky toward the ground. Shivering from the cold, he winced as he struggled with the controls. The engine was trying to stall. Every move made his chest throb from the cracked ribs he'd received a few days earlier.

Hundreds of gallons of liquid oxygen fueled the X-1, or the orange beast as the crew liked to call her. He might as well be riding a bomb, Chuck thought. Despite the odds, this brave pilot wasn't frightened. Not the cold, not the pain from the cracked ribs, not a stalled engine, and not even the threat of a fiery death would keep him from flying supersonic. More than anything, he wanted to prove that there was no natural barrier to supersonic flight.

The moment the nose turned, the plane began to pick up speed. Chuck fired the rockets and climbed to 36,000 feet at .88 Mach. At 40,000 feet, the X-1 reached .92 Mach. After another short rocket boost, the X-1 reached .96 Mach. Could the sound barrier really be just seconds away? He noticed that the faster the X-1 went, the smoother the ride got.

Suddenly, the speed gauge began to fluctuate. Once the plane reached .965 Mach, the needle went completely off the scale. Chuck tapped the gauge, but the needle stuck firm—far off the scale.

Zooming along, he prepared to hit that invisible wall known as the sound barrier, but that never seemed to happen. Instead of bursting into flames, he finally slowed the plane down after a very smooth 20-second flight. Then, he radioed the B-29 to report the gauge problem. Just then, one of the ground crew also radioed in to report hearing a distant boom that sounded like thunder. Later, they would all come to realize that the ground crew had heard the very first sonic boom.

Back on the ground, Chuck learned that the first supersonic flight—his flight—had reached 1.07 Mach. He was elated. He hadn't expected such a smooth ride. The plane hadn't flown apart. There was no explosion. He had beat the odds and been the first to break the sound barrier.

FYInfo
FOR YOUR INFORMATION

The Sound Barrier

The X1 and the B-29

As an aircraft approaches the speed of sound, approximately 761 miles per hour, the increased pressure compresses the air into a liquid. That puts stress on the craft. Experts once thought that it would be impossible to travel faster than the speed of sound. They theorized that a craft flying the speed of sound would disintegrate. Many referred to this phenomenon as the sound barrier.

The real problem was that the aircraft of the day weren't designed to withstand the added pressure of supersonic flight. Chuck Yeager's historic flight smashed the sound barrier theory once and for all.

The actual speed of sound differs depending on the air temperature. At high altitudes the temperature is much colder. That means the higher you fly, the slower sound travels. In addition, the medium through which the craft is moving—fresh water, salt water, and our atmosphere—changes the speed of sound.

The following is a simplified formula for calculating the approximate speed of sound in our atmosphere:

speed of sound = 761 + (0.6 x T)

where T equals the temperature in Celsius. Convert Fahrenheit to Celsius using this formula

(Ft - 32) x (5/9)

where Ft is the degrees in Fahrenheit.

Supersonic speeds are measured in Mach numbers. Once you know the speed of sound, you can easily determine the Mach number using this formula:

actual speed ÷ the speed of sound

An aircraft traveling at 693 miles per hour where the speed of sound is 770 is traveling .9 Mach. If you know the Mach number, calculate the actual speed using this formula:

Mach Number x the speed of sound

For instance, a .9 Mach flight equals 693 miles per hour where the speed of sound equals 770 miles per hour. All of these formulas are only for aircraft flying in our own atmosphere.

Chuck Yeager was one of many Air Forc
the X-1 experimental aircraft.

The X-1 couldn't launch itself from a runway, so a specially modified B-29 bomber carried the experimental aircraft into flight. At 20,000 feet, the bomber dropped the X-1 into open air where the pilot fired the rockets so the aircraft could fly on its own. Eventually, the small craft would glide to a landing on the desert floor.

CHAPTER 2

A Country Boy

"Well Chuck, why are you late this time?" the principal asked.

Chuck answered, "I was hunting this morning and I just lost track of the time."

It was mostly the truth. Chuck often rose before dawn to go hunting. He would shoot several squirrels or rabbits for the family's supper. Times were tough and he didn't mind providing supper. If there were no squirrels or rabbits, he'd go fishing instead. He never meant to be late, but to Chuck, supper was more important than the morning's first lesson.

All the kids in Hamlin, West Virginia, knew how to hunt. Nobody was better at it than Chuck. He could spot a squirrel or rabbit before anyone else. Although he didn't know it at the time, he had 20/10 vision. A person with 20/10 vision can see twice as far as the average person. Those special eyes would help him become a great fighter pilot later in life.

Charles Elwood Yeager was born on February 13, 1923, in West Virginia to Albert and Susie Yeager. Growing up during the Great Depression in the Appalachian foothills with several siblings was rough. (One of Chuck's younger sisters died as a toddler.)

His parents were loving and responsible. The Yeagers taught their children the value of being honest and doing a good job. One of Chuck's first jobs was capping bottles of home-brewed beer and wine for his father.

Chuck's dad was an expert mechanic and worked hard in his natural gas drilling business. From early on, machinery fascinated young Chuck. Thanks to his dad, he learned all about generators and pumps. In fact, he spent a good deal of his childhood helping his dad in the field and repairing his drilling equipment.

Chuck's mom was loving, but firm. Respect for elders was very important to her. She took her kids to church and made them walk the straight and narrow path. Most of all, Susie Yeager loved her family and worked hard to provide for them during difficult times.

Money was tight, but Chuck grew up happy. He was loved and well cared for.

His parents taught by example, and they were both hard workers. Albert and Susie Yeager always did the best they could with what they had, and they didn't complain. Working alongside both his parents, Chuck learned to work hard and to do his best. His eagerness to do the best job he could served him well all of his life.

Childhood wasn't all work and struggle. When he wasn't in school or helping around at home, he was thrashing through the woods or swimming in the Mud River. He loved being outdoors—summer, fall, winter, and spring.

He graduated from Hamlin High School where he excelled in math in the spring of 1941. He spent that summer working in a pool hall, even though his dad didn't approve of the job.

"Son, don't gamble," said Chuck's dad when Chuck joined the Army Air Corps in the summer of 1941.[1] The new recruit wanted to be an airplane mechanic. It was the logical choice. After helping his dad drill in the fields all those years, he was a skilled mechanic. He could take an entire car engine apart and put it back together again, with no help.

Unlike most of the young men in Chuck's outfit, he didn't know anything about flying an airplane. In fact, flying made him sick. He threw up during his first few flights. However, he forgot all about his flight sickness when he read about the Flying Sergeant Program. His high school diploma was his quick ticket to making Sergeant. Before the Flying Sergeants Program, hopeful pilots had to have a college degree. (Chuck never went to college.)

Most of the recruits wanted to fly. Chuck wanted to be a Sergeant, and didn't mind that he'd have to fly to be promoted. He received word that he was moving to the Flying Sergeant Program a few months before the Japanese bombed Pearl Harbor. He began actual flight training in early 1942. He was surprised to discover that he loved to fly.

After training, he received his wings and reported to the 363rd Fighter Squadron in Nevada, as a non-commissioned flight officer. Like everything else in his life, he set out to be the best, and he succeeded. He constantly pushed the limits by flying more and flying harder than any other pilot did. Within a few months, everyone knew that Chuck was one of the best new pilots in the squadron.

Flying was all he wanted to do. Nothing could've made him happier than he was—or at least he thought so at the time. Eventually, the squadron made their way to Oroville, California, which proved to be a fateful move for Chuck. It was there that he met and fell in love with his future wife.

Soon after arriving in Oroville, Chuck asked the local USO's Social Director, Glennis Dickhouse, to plan a dance. Glennis made all the arrangements and even attended the dance with Chuck. Over the next several months, Glennis and Chuck saw each other a lot.

The United States entered World War II on December 7, 1941, when the Japanese bombed Pearl Harbor, Hawaii. By that time, the majority of the world's nations were already involved. Fighting occurred all over the globe and the toll was huge—about 55.5 million people lost their lives in the war. There were two groups; the Allies, which included the United States, Great Britain, the Soviet Union, China, France, Poland, and other European countries occupied by the Axis, which included Germany, Italy, Japan, and their allies.

With the threat of war looming between them, Chuck and Glennis both knew their days together were numbered. They knew the country was at war; they knew that being a fighter pilot was dangerous work. Soon Chuck would be on his way overseas and to war. They didn't discuss marriage or make any promises to one another. Nothing could've prepared the two for what happened to Chuck next.

Chuck married Glennis as soon as he returned from his combat mission in Europe.

Chuck and Glennis met in California while Chuck was in flight school in 1942. He thought she was the most beautiful woman he'd ever seen. They remained married until Glennis' death in 1990. She fully supported Chuck's career through their entire marriage.

FYInfo

For Your Information

Growing up During the Great Depression

America's Great Depression was the worst economic slump the United States has ever known. Beginning in late 1929, the slump lasted for more than a decade. Most families had little money because work was hard to find. Often, just finding enough to eat was difficult. Families that lived in the country, like Chuck's family, had an easier time because they could grow their own food and hunt for game.

A number of factors contributed to the Great Depression. During the twenties, the economy was unstable. People borrowed money to speculate in the stock market and businesses made unwise investments. By far, the most damaging event was the stock market crash of 1929.

The crash heard 'round the world occurred on October 29, 1929—Black Tuesday. By the end of the day, a lot of people had lost everything. Rich businessmen were left in ruin. Whole companies shut their doors overnight, putting ordinary people out of work. Americans suddenly had no money to spend, which affected markets all over the world.

Franklin D. Roosevelt is credited with holding our country together during the Great Depression.

In March 1933, the new president, Franklin D. Roosevelt, took over a nation in despair. Then, there was a run on the banks. That means that people withdrew their savings. Too many people tried to withdraw too much on the same day and some of the banks ran out of cash. You see, your money isn't really in the bank in some cold vault. The bank lends your money to help families buy homes and to help businesses to expand. In return, the bank pays you interest on your savings.

Roosevelt made a bold move. He declared a bank holiday and shut the banks for three days. When the banks reopened, people had calmed down a bit and the crisis had passed. About this time, the federal government established the Federal Deposit Insurance Corporation (FDIC), which still insures bank deposits today. Should a bank fail, this corporation reimburses depositors a percentage of their losses. The United States was finally recovering from the Great Depression when Chuck entered the service.

Chuck Yeager flew over 180 different t
during his career, including this F-100

Chuck started his flying career in a P-51 Mustang during combat in World War II. As a test pilot his service was vital in helping the Air Force develop the fastest jet fighters in the world.

CHAPTER 3

Behind Enemy Lines and Back Again

Chuck saw the German planes too late. The gunfire and explosion seemed to come at once. His plane rolled, and suddenly, he was falling through the busted canopy and spinning through open air toward the ground—southern France to be exact.

After bouncing off the top of a huge pine tree, a limb caught his parachute. He hung from the trees, just a few inches from the ground. Only after freeing himself from the snagged parachute, did he notice the blood dripping from both his leg and his head. German soldiers were pursuing him and he was wounded.

It was March 5, 1944. One minute Chuck was flying one of 16 P-51 Mustangs as an air escort for B-24s on a bombing run. The next minute, he was wounded and looking for a hiding place in occupied territory.

The situation was desperate, but he reacted quickly and soundly, as he always did. His only hope was to find a friendly local before the Germans found him. For a while, he'd have to sit tight. He quickly hid in the deep forest brush.

The next morning, the Germans were gone and Chuck crawled from his hiding spot. Eventually, he spotted a woodcutter. He ran at the woodcutter, waving his pistol. "Me American. Need help. Find underground." Chuck demanded of the frightened Frenchman.[1]

The P-51 is much smaller than most modern jet fighters, but she was extremely fast and maneuverable.

Chuck's famous sound-barrier breaking flight proved once and for all that there is no natural barrier to flying faster than sound. Today, some planes are designed specifically for supersonic flight.

An hour later, Chuck was on his way to safety. He spent the next two weeks recovering from his wounds on a French farm. He couldn't hide from the Germans forever. Every day he stayed at the farm was a dangerous day for him and his new French friends. If the Germans discovered him, they would send him to a prisoner of war camp. Unfortunately, the French farm family was in much more danger. The Germans would shoot them on the spot.

Back home, Chuck was reported as missing in action. Mrs. Yeager called Glennis and broke the bad news. They waited for a month for news of Chuck.

One night he was taken into the forest. He and his French friends spent the next two days in the forest, traveling deeper and deeper into the mountains. Eventually, his new friends turned him over to the Marquis.

The Marquis were a brave group of French civilians who were opposed to the German occupation. They used guerilla warfare tactics to undermine the Germans wherever, however they could. They blew up bridges, trains, and German camps. They even assassinated German officials and French citizens that were helpful to the Germans.

Because of the danger, the Marquis hid all day and fought at night. They all knew being captured meant sudden death. Despite the danger, they fought the Germans. They wanted their country back.

Chuck traveled with the Marquis for a few weeks, but he never went on any missions with them. One night, he did stand watch while an English bomber dropped supplies into an open field. In the dropped bundle, they found weapons, ammunition, explosives, and triggers. Some of the instructions were in English, so Chuck showed them how to use the fuses and set the different timers. Most likely, he didn't even need the instructions. He'd learned all about explosives, fuses, and triggers from his father.

Living with the Marquis was dangerous for Chuck. The Geneva Convention, an agreement that protected prisoners of war, protected him as long as he was acting as an American soldier. Captured soldiers were sent to a prisoner of war camp. If the Germans found him with the Marquis, they would shoot him on the spot. He needed to make his way to Spain, which was a neutral country during World War II. The Spanish couldn't send him back to his squadron—doing so would violate their neutral status. He would have to sit out the war in Spain, but at least the Spanish wouldn't shoot him or send him to a prisoner of war camp.

Even if he made it back, his fighter pilot days were most likely over. The allies wouldn't take the chance of sending him back into combat. If he were recaptured, the Germans would torture him to get information about the Marquis.

One night, a couple of Marquis members walked Chuck into a small French village. He was frightened. How could they take such chances? The village was full of German soldiers. What he didn't know at the time was that another group of Marquis was waiting inside the village for him. Later that night, the new group drove him to the foot of the Pyrenees Mountains, where he joined a small group of Americans.

Roughly three weeks after he was shot down, Chuck and a few other Americans began their journey over the snow-covered mountains and into Spain. It was March 23, 1944. Snow had fallen and the higher they climbed, the colder it grew. The air grew thinner, and the travelers had to stop frequently to rest. Sometimes they could walk for only 15 to 20 minutes before they grew so tired they had to stop. The frequent stops and the knee-high snow and ice made for a long, treacherous and miserable journey. Not everyone made it across the mountains alive.

Four days into the trip, Chuck and his lone companion, a navigator named Patterson, were too exhausted to continue. Their feet were numb from frostbite. They spotted a small cabin in the snow. It was dangerous to stop, but they couldn't go any further without rest. They approached the cabin cautiously, and found it empty. Inside, they both collapsed into a deep sleep. The situation was grim, but it was about to get even worse.

Chuck awoke to gunfire—a German patrol was shooting at them through the front door. Chuck and Pat (as Chuck called him) leapt out a back window, but not soon enough. A bullet struck Pat. Chuck grabbed him and jumped over the side of a ridge, dragging Pat with him. Together, they slid straight down the side of that mountain. It's probably what saved them because the German soldiers were hundreds of feet above them—straight up the side of a mountain. It would take the Germans a while to catch up to them.

Pat was unconscious and seriously wounded. After tying up the wound, Chuck waited. After dark, he began a journey that few men would attempt. He dragged Pat, unconscious, back up the ridge, inch by inch. The climb took all night.

The next morning, Chuck, still pulling Pat, crossed over the top of the ridge and into Spain. It was March 28, 1944—they'd spent five cold days in the mountains.

Eventually, Pat's leg was amputated and the Spanish sent him home. Chuck, on the other hand, went to jail. The Spanish authorities really had nowhere else to put him.

Never one to be stymied by a challenge, he simply escaped from jail. Later that same day, he found a small hotel, called a pestione in Spain, just a few blocks from the jail. He ate, he took a hot bath, and then he slept for two days in a real bed.

On March 30, 1944, the American consul took him to a Spanish resort. Less than a month after being shot down over enemy territory, he was resting and waiting in safety.

He was in a nice hotel in a warm little village and the consul was paying all of his expenses. He took advantage of the time by resting and eating well. Most people would've been content to sit out the rest of the war, but not Chuck. Once he recovered his health, he was ready to get back to his buddies and the war.

The American consul finally negotiated a deal to smuggle Chuck and several other American servicemen out of Spain. After six weeks of resting under the Spanish sun, the Spanish traded him for a few barrels of gasoline, and he was on his way back to England and his fighter squadron.

Back in England, the Army Air Corps awarded Chuck the Bronze Star for saving Pat's life. But he was unhappy because he was going back to the states. Once again, he took charge of the present and secured his future—he refused to go home.

That summer, the war in Europe was winding down. After the invasion of Normandy in June, the Marquis switched from guerilla tactics to open battle. The Marquis had exposed themselves, so Chuck no longer was a threat to their safety. He was also the first evadee (trooper to make it back from behind enemy lines) to make it all the way back to his squadron. Things had changed and there was no reason to keep him out of combat. At least that's how he felt about it.

The next few weeks were a series of meetings and lots of waiting as Chuck marched up the chain of command. He tried hard to convince them to let him stay in England with his squadron. That march took him all the way to the top of the chain—to General Dwight Eisenhower.

"General," Chuck said, "I don't want to leave my buddies after only eight missions. It just isn't right. I have a lot of fighting left to do."[2] General Eisenhower promised to turn the matter over to Washington, D.C. A few days later, Chuck's orders home were canceled. He had convinced the general to let him stay. He rejoined his squadron and returned to the war during the summer of 1944. He named his second plane Glamorous Glen II.

By the end of September, Chuck was a group leader of three squadrons. On October 12, he shot down five enemy planes and became the first pilot to become a flying ace in one day. That accomplishment earned him a Silver Star. His 20/10 eyesight gave him a huge advantage because he could see the enemy planes before the enemy pilots could spot him.

Another history-making day for Chuck came soon after his promotion when he became the first pilot to shoot down one of Germany's new jet fighters, an Me262. Pilots found it impossible to get a Mustang close enough because the jets were so fast. When Chuck spotted three of those new jets flying below him, he just followed them home.

As the jet approached the landing strip, he dove straight in at 500 miles per hour. He let off a quick round of gunfire and then climbed quickly to escape the flak coming from the ground. The German jet crashed and burned seconds after his surprise attack. He won the Distinguished Flying Cross for being the first American pilot to shoot down a German jet.

Glamorous Glen III is just one of five planes named for his wife Glennis. To celebrate the 50th anniversary of his famous flight, he flew a brand new F-15 Eagle named Glamorous Glennis.

Chuck named his planes for his wife Glennis.

By age 22, Chuck was an ace fighter pilot, a Captain in the Air Corps, a group leader, his squadron's maintenance officer, the winner of several battle honors, and his tour—now flying Glamorous Glen III—was about over. He'd flown 64 combat missions and logged 270 hours in three different Mustangs, all named for Glennis, his fiancé. By April 1945, he was stationed at Perrin Field, Texas, with his new bride, the real Glamorous Glennis. Life should've been grand for the Yeager's, but they were miserable. There was no place for the couple to live, and Chuck hated his job as a pilot instructor.

A new regulation allowed evadees to pick their own assignment. Chuck chose Wright Field in Dayton, Ohio, because it was so close to his home in Hamlin. With a baby on the way, the Yeager's wanted to be close to family.

Unfortunately, Chuck's plan had a flaw. The Yeager's couldn't find a decent place to live in Dayton. Despite Chuck's best intentions, Glennis ended up in Hamlin with his family instead of in Dayton with him.

Building a family and a career put Chuck at odds with himself. He missed Glennis, but he could fly all he wanted, and he was having a blast. Being stationed at Wright Field was one of the best career decisions he ever made—even though he didn't know it at the time.

The Yeager's had four children who traveled the world with them.

Chuck's older son Donald was also a pilot in the Air Force. They both served together in Southeast Asia during the Vietnam War. Donald was a pilot; Chuck was a bird colonel commanding the 405th Fighter Wing.

FYInfo
For Your Information

A Day in the Life of a Fighter Pilot

Chuck in fighter pilot gear

Conditions were harsh at the tiny airstrip in England where Chuck was stationed in 1944. There was no hot water, no heat, or air conditioning, and meals were often cold and out of a can. Days started at five thirty in the morning. After shaving in cold water, Chuck attended a briefing about the day's mission.

Flight gear included two pairs of wool socks and fleece-lined boots. The cockpit's small heater kept it just warm enough to prevent frostbite. The average temperature outside the cockpit was 60 degrees below zero (Fahrenheit).

Chuck also wore a standard issue forty-five (a pistol), a leather flight jacket, a Mae West, a parachute, a leather flight helmet, and goggles. A Mae West was a life vest preserver named for a buxom blonde actress who was popular during the first half of the twentieth century.

A Mustang fighter had no bathroom. Since the average mission was six hours long, the pilots went to the bathroom just before boarding their planes. The ride home was miserable enough for the pilot without adding the discomfort of holding his bladder or bowels.

By eight o'clock, the planes were roaring down the runway. Once in the air, they fastened an oxygen mask and began their climb to around 28,000 feet. They would spend the next six hours in the cold, cramped cockpit.

Once home, the hungry pilots went in search of a hot meal, having missed lunch while they were gone. If they were lucky, they had enough energy to walk or ride a bike into the nearest village and grab a warm supper at a pub. Otherwise, they were left to whatever they could scrounge from their private stock, perhaps a cold Spam sandwich. Exhausted, the pilots fell into bed only to wake up the next morning and do it all over again.

Among the many aircraft that Chuck
stands posed in front of an F-86 Sabr

Chuck had more flying time than almost any other pilot in history. He loved flying and took every opportunity to fly—in any craft, at any time.

Breaking the Sound Barrier

In July 1945, Chuck was the new Assistant Maintenance Officer to the Flight Test Division at Wright Field. He wasn't a test pilot, but he got plenty of flying time just the same. He flew because he loved to, but ultimately all that flying meant he had more time and experience in more planes than just about any other pilot. Nobody logged more time flying than Chuck.

His mechanical background kicked into overdrive and not only did he fly everything he could, he explored their engines. The planes were like a second skin for him—he knew what every sound and vibration meant. He knew how to push each engine to its limits, and he knew how to respond when there was trouble.

Chuck wasn't building his career, he just loved to fly. Just the same, all that experience with so many different aircraft made him the perfect choice for overseeing the maintenance of the Lockheed P-80 Shooting Star—America's first operational jet fighter.

Four months after arriving at Wright Field, he was picked to fly the new jet at the Wright Field Open-House Air Show over several dozen other test pilots. His commander was so impressed with his expert piloting skills that within days he was in test pilot training.

Around this time, Yeager's first child, Donald, was born. He was two weeks old before Chuck saw him for the first time. Oddly enough, he really believed that life would settle down after he completed test pilot school. Once again, his life was about to change, and he didn't even see it coming.

The Lockheed P-80 Shooting Star was America's first operational jet fighter.

Chuch Yeager earned the attention of Colonel Albert Boyd for his skill of flying and his mechnical knowledge of all types of aircraft. Chuck flew the Lockheed P-80 more than most pilots and gained valuable experience during his time as a maintenance officer.

Shortly after completing test pilot school, Chuck was selected to be the first pilot to fly the new X-S-1 experimental aircraft through the sound barrier (the S, which was eventually dropped, stood for supersonic). The choice was radical. He was still an inexperienced test pilot. There were dozens of more qualified and more experienced test pilots. Just the same, the brass (Chuck's bosses) saw something in Chuck that they liked. Repeatedly, he had proven that he could handle any engine and any crisis. More importantly, he never panicked. He pushed a craft to its limits, but he used good sense and knew exactly when to pull back. Instinctively, he seemed to know what an aircraft could do, and perhaps more importantly, what it couldn't do. He was definitely the best pilot for the job.

Chuck didn't know much about the sound barrier and its potential dangers, but he knew he wanted the job. He spent his workweek at

Muroc Air Base in California and flew home to be with his family on the weekends. It was tough on his family, especially since they had a brand new baby boy named Mickey. Despite the danger, Glennis fully supported Chuck's choice.

Everyone involved with the project knew how dangerous it was, but Chuck was excited to be flying such an incredible aircraft. Initially, the X-1 couldn't launch itself from the ground. To compensate, the small X-1 dangled from the belly of a specially rigged B-29 bomber. The bomb bay doors had been removed and Chuck entered the X-1's cockpit through the B-29's bomber bay. When the B-29 reached 12,000 feet, he slid down a ladder into the X-1's cockpit. It was unsafe for him to board any sooner than that. If the X-1 was accidentally released below 10,000 feet, both the ship and Chuck would've been lost. They could rebuild the X-1, but they couldn't rebuild him.

Once inside the cockpit, he locked the X-1's door. At about 25,000 feet, the bomber would drop the X-1, and Chuck, into open sky.

The first flight was fuel-less. He glided the beast to a dry lakebed in the desert below. It was flawless and lasted only a few minutes. He believed the X-1 was the best plane he'd ever flown.

The first fueled flight was on August 29, 1947. Six hundred gallons of liquid oxygen filled the tanks. There was no heater in the cockpit, so it was miserably cold. But dealing with the cold was the easy part. Liquid oxygen is highly volatile. The X-1 was little more than a bomb with a passenger seat. In fact, the fueled ship was so dangerous that the base was closed down for the first fueled flight. Only once the plane was safely in the air did the base reopen.

Fueled flights weren't as smooth as the first three glided missions had been, at least not at first. The B-29's speed was too slow on the first fueled fight. Chuck knew he was in trouble as soon as the X-1 was dropped. The B-29 had been going too slow and the X-1 tried to stall.

This possibility was exactly why Chuck has been picked from all the other test pilots. He didn't panic. Instead, he fought with the controls until the X-1 responded. Once in control, he fired the first rocket. The force slammed him into the back of his seat and he was off.

He began to climb at .7 Mach. At 45,000 feet, he left the morning sky behind and flew to the edge of space. He was so excited that he got a bit carried away and disobeyed orders. He was supposed to jettison any fuel that was left and then glide back to a safe lakebed landing. Instead, at a speed of .8 Mach and only 300 feet off the ground, he buzzed the air base. He got chewed out for the unplanned trip. From then on, he followed the flight plan, but he never forgot the thrill of that first fueled flight.

Chuck's team learned from each flight. After each flight, they studied all the data and made adjustments to the equipment. Chuck pushed the X-1 just a little faster each flight. He found that at .86 Mach the beast was hard to control and sluggish.

The first time he reached .97 Mach the beast wouldn't respond to the controls. Back at the base, the engineers made adjustments, but no one was sure they'd work until Chuck ran a test flight. Luck—or perhaps it was good old ingenuity—was with them and the adjustments worked. He was able to take her to .96 Mach, the very next flight. However, that flight wasn't trouble-free. After jettisoning his remaining fuel so he could land, the windshield frosted over. Chuck couldn't see to land! His chase man, Dick Frost, talked him through the landing. The chase man flew above the beast to observe each flight from above the X-1.

Back on the ground, the crew worked to solve the frost problem. After a little experimenting, they started coating the windshield with a special formula before each flight.[1] That special formula turned out to be a popular dandruff shampoo (Drene shampoo).

Exhaustion was setting in and they all needed a break. The following weekend Chuck took Glennis horseback riding at Pancho Barnes' ranch. Pancho and Chuck were the best of friends, and the X-1 crew spent a lot of time at Pancho's ranch.

Pancho Barnes had been a Hollywood stunt pilot and civilian test pilot. There weren't many women flying airplanes back then. Many thought

Pancho Barnes and Chuck became friends for life while he was testing the X-1. She had an inn near the base and the pilots and crew spent a lot of time there unwinding and relaxing.

Pancho Barnes was one of the only female pilots of the time.

Pancho behaved outrageously. Even so, she was one of the best pilots in the world. By her mid forties, she was running a dude ranch named "Pancho's Flying Inn" in the Mojave Desert. Chuck and the X-1 crew spent a lot of time relaxing at her ranch.

It was at Pancho's ranch that Chuck took a fall when his horse ran into a fence. The fall broke two of his ribs, but he refused to go to the base hospital. He knew his commander would ground him. The next morning, a local doctor taped his ribs.

Chuck arrived at the base at six o'clock on the morning of October 14, 1947, as if nothing had happened. Two hours later at eight o'clock, the B-29 carrying the X-1 took off. The day's flight would be the ninth fueled flight. He knew they were close to breaking the sound barrier. Today might be the day.

Right out of the B-29, the X-1 wanted to stall. When Chuck finally gained control he fired all four rockets and climbed to 36,000 feet going .88 Mach. He took her to 40,000 feet at .92 Mach. At 42,000 feet he reached .96 Mach. He noticed that the harder he pushed, the smoother the ride got.

Then, the speed gauge needle began to fluctuate. Twenty seconds later, he radioed Jack Ridley, the chase man.

"Hey Ridley, that Machmeter is acting screwy. It just went off the scale on me."

"Fluctuated off?"

"Yeah, at point nine-six-five."

"Son, you is imagining things."

"Must be. I'm still wearing my ears and nothing else fell off, neither."[2]

None of them knew that Chuck had indeed broken the sound barrier—not yet. Just then the crew in the tracking van reported the loud distant thunder. Later, he would learn that the beast had reached 1.07 Mach.

Oddly enough, breaking the sound barrier was a bit of a let down for Chuck. He had prepared for turbulence. He had expected some kind of physical shock, but the ride had been smooth. If the meter hadn't fluctuated, he would not have known that anything was different. He had flown at supersonic speed and not even known it, for sure, until data later confirmed the flight's top speed.

Back on the ground, the crew was excited, but there was no base party to celebrate. The brass insisted that the crew keep the flight quiet. No one but Chuck's crew and the Air Force knew that Chuck had finally broken the sound barrier. No one would know about their history-making flight for almost another year. Washington, D.C., awarded him another Distinguished Flying Cross in a top-secret ceremony just a week later. Chuck remained modest, as always.

"Aw, shucks, I just happened to be at the right place at the right time. It was no big deal. Just another job."[3]

You might think that breaking the sound barrier was the end of the X-1 project, but it was really just the beginning. Chuck continued to fly the beast at high altitudes. The more he pushed, the more dangerous the project became for him. Although everyone had confidence in the X-1, it was still an experimental aircraft.

Just two weeks after breaking the sound barrier, Chuck had a close call. He couldn't ignite the rockets; he couldn't jettison the fuel. There was no radio to call for help. He was plummeting to an explosive death. Fortunately, Dick Frost, the project's engineer, had foreseen this possibility. He had added a manual valve to release the fuel, just in case. Chuck remembered the valve, but he had no way of knowing whether the manual release was really working—there was no gauge. All he could do was hope. In the end, he delayed the landing as long as possible in order to drop as much fuel as possible. The landing was successful thanks to Dick's ingenuity and foresight and Chuck's calm reaction to the crisis.

A few weeks later Chuck had another close call when the B-29's release cord didn't work. There he was hanging in the X-1 from the B-29's belly. The release cord wouldn't budge, and the B-29 was forced to land with the X-1 still attached. That meant Chuck had to climb out of the X-1 and back into the B-29. Had the release cord suddenly snapped while he was climbing out, he had no place to go but down. Once again, he beat the odds and the B-29 landed with no damage to the X-1 or to him.

During post-barrier-breaking flights, the release cord continued to be a problem. On another flight the rockets wouldn't ignite right away. Several flights ended early because of small fires in the engine. Despite problems, Chuck pushed the X-1 to 1.35 Mach (890 miles per hour).

As he climbed higher, he had to wear a pressurized flight suit. He was closing the gap between man and space well before the space program existed.

In February and March 1948, the engine caught fire several times. For the first time, Chuck was truly afraid. He had nightmares of being burned alive in the X-1. Eventually, an engineer discovered the problem and it was fixed. Chuck had flown 23 fueled missions and his commanders decided that enough was enough.

He remained with the X-1, but not as the test pilot. Several new test pilots took their rides over the next year. None of them was ever as comfortable flying the X-1 as Chuck had been.

Finally, in June 1948, the Air Force announced Chuck's historic flight. President Harry S. Truman awarded him the Collier Trophy. The Collier Trophy is the most important award given to members of the aviation community. Suddenly, Chuck was very popular. He spent a lot of his time giving speeches instead of testing the X-1. He wasn't happy about that change, but he obeyed orders.

Hans Guido Mutke, a German pilot, also claimed to have flown the sound of speed on April 9, 1945 (during combat). In a steep dive with the engine at full power, his Messerschmitt Me262 began to shake uncontrollably. He reduced the power and only after landing found that his plane was missing many rivets and that the wings were damaged. After Mutke learned of Chuck Yeager's historic flight, he realized that he might have reached supersonic speed on that 1945 flight. Unfortunately for Mutke, there was no way to prove his claim.

On January 5, 1949, Chuck took the X-1 out for a spin, launching from the runway for the first time. By now, the program was nearing its end. Thanks to Chuck's flight, the myth of the sound barrier could be put to rest. That flight proved once and for all that there was no physical barrier to flying faster than the speed of sound. The real barrier was bad aerodynamic design. An aircraft could fly at supersonic speed if the aircraft was aerodynamically sound.

From 1947 to 1949 Chuck flew the X-1, also known as Glamorous Glen, 33 times. (Chuck named his planes Glamorous Glen and Glamorous Glennis.) He flew her faster than anyone else, reaching 1.45 Mach (957 miles per hour). The X-1 was retired to the Smithsonian Institute in Washington, D.C., in 1950. Other famous aircraft on display include the Spirit of St. Louis, the Apollo 11 module, and a Concorde jet. Supersonic travel was now a real possibility. Chuck and Washington, D.C., looked beyond the experimental aircraft, and they saw the next frontier, outer space.

The Orange Beast

The X-1

The X-1 was a research aircraft with a rocket engine built by the Bell Aircraft Corporation for the United States Army Air Corps (which later became the United States Air Force). Its fuselage was shaped like a bullet and the wings were straight with a span of 28 feet. The bullet-shaped fuselage was 30 feet and 11 inches. The craft weighed 14,751 pounds. Originally, the craft was called the X-S-1 (Experimental, Supersonic, and first).

Chuck's main mission was to test the aircraft at transonic speeds. Transonic is the range just below to just above the speed of sound. There were three X-1s and 18 pilots flying them from 1946 to 1951. Chuck wasn't the first to fly the X-1. Bell's test pilot flew the X-1 ten times before turning it over to Chuck. All ten of those flights were unpowered subsonic flights.

The X-1 was fueled by liquid oxygen, which is extremely cold, but nonflammable. However, it is an oxidizer, which means that anything that will burn will burn more quickly and hotter if burning in liquid oxygen. Fire was a constant threat.

Liquid oxygen boils at -297.3 degrees Fahrenheit. That means it's very difficult to insulate liquid oxygen because there's such a difference between the stored liquid oxygen and the surrounding environment. Special cryogenic tanks kept the liquid oxygen very cold. Although liquid oxygen is not toxic, humans must limit their exposure to it. It irritates the respiratory system and can cause complications such as coughing, nasal stuffiness, sore throat, and chest pain after just a few hours. Continued exposure can cause worse symptoms such as tracheobronchitis, pulmonary congestion, and edema, which are lung disease, heart trouble, and bad circulation.

Testing of the X-1 led to many structural and aerodynamic improvements in future aircraft.

Chuck continued to fly and serve as a consultant after retiring.

Chuck's flying career didn't stop after he retired. Chuck continues to fly all over the country speaking to groups and appearing at aviation functions.

The End is Just the Beginning

After breaking the sound barrier, the last place Chuck expected to find himself was back in flight school. Unfortunately for him, he hadn't actually finished test pilot school. After finishing the first half, he immediately began testing the X-1. Now, the Air Force demanded he tackle the second half. If he didn't, he was through as a test pilot.

The other pilots in the program resented him and called him a hillbilly because he spoke with a heavy accent. He didn't have a college degree, and they were angry that he'd been chosen to test the X-1 over an educated pilot with more experience. The instructors even tried to fail him after he missed several days of class on a special mission. Chuck worried that his test piloting days were really over.

It just so happened that the school's commanding officer was none other than General Albert Boyd, who had originally chosen Chuck for the X-1 program. General Boyd knew that Chuck knew as much if not more than most of the instructors at the school. It was clear to the general that Chuck wasn't getting a fair deal. He demanded that the instructors give him a fair assessment. Chuck passed the second half of test pilot training.

Technology changed quickly over the next few years. Chuck got to test a number of new jets. In December 1953 he was nearly killed in one. At 80,000 feet, he was higher than planned in the X-1A and running at 2.44 Mach. (He broke the current speed record by traveling 1,650 miles per hour that day.) Just then, the plane began to roll and he lost control of the craft, which began to spin horizontally. He was tossed around the cockpit and momentarily stunned. He thought he was going to die.

Colonel Albert Boyd stands beside his P-80R Shooting Star.

During his career, Major General Albert Boyd had clocked 23,000 flying hours and had flown several hundred different types of aircraft. For his oustanding accomplishments, he also received the Legion of Merit and Distinguished Flying Cross.

Instead, as Chuck always did, he focused on the job, trusted his instincts, and managed to flip the spin at 30,000 feet. For the next 5,000 feet, he spun toward the ground in a vertical spin. At 25,000 feet he recovered the plane. A few minutes later, he landed in the desert. That morning, he plummeted 51,000 feet in 51 seconds. The speed record Chuck broke that morning wasn't broken for another three years.

President Eisenhower presented Major Yeager the Harmon Trophy in 1954 for his flight in the X-1A. About the same time, fate stepped in. The Pentagon removed Chuck from the test piloting program. Even they knew his luck had to run out soon. He was too valuable to them to lose. They needed his experience.

In 1954, Chuck began his next assignment. He was 32 years old and commanding a squadron of fighter pilots nearly as old as he was. His

Chuck's most serious accident occurred in the X-1A experimental aircraft. He was seriously burned and spent a month in the hospital.

As a colonel, Chuck continued to fly with his men.

squadron, the 417th Fighter Squadron, stationed in Hahn, Germany, was one of the first to carry nuclear bombs.

By 1962, he was a colonel and running the new USAF Aerospace Research Pilot School, training astronauts. Once again, he was on the cutting edge of the military aviation world.

He managed to find a bit of trouble in his new position. Bobby Kennedy, the Attorney General, encouraged a black aviator named Ed Dwight to apply to the school. Unfortunately, he ranked twenty-fifth on the admission test. The class took only the top 11. Despite Dwight's ranking, the White House intervened on his behalf and Chuck admitted him to the school.

Ed passed the course, but NASA didn't accept him into their program. As a result, Chuck found himself in the middle of a congressional investigation. Charges of discrimination were made against him and the school. Eventually, the investigation was dropped because no evidence of discrimination was found.

Despite Ed's early disappointment, he became the first black aviator to train as an astronaut. After retiring from the Air Force in 1966, he became a famous sculptor.

Running a school didn't keep Chuck out of physical danger. In 1963, he took an NF-104 Starfighter up to 104,000 feet. The plane went into a spin and he couldn't recover. He eventually ejected. On the way down the seat hit his head. Burning debris on the seat ignited and he was consumed by flames. He lived, but spent the next month in the hospital. The jump was another first for Chuck. He was the first to eject wearing a pressure suit.

He never did fly in space, but he did train the first generation of young astronauts.

In 1966, Chuck was a bird colonel and commanding the 405th Fighter Wing in Southeast Asia. Both he and his oldest son Donald were serving in Vietnam at the same time. During this time, he usually flew a B-57 light bomber, and he logged 414 hours of combat time. Most colonels didn't fly combat missions, but Chuck insisted on flying with his men.

Chuck learned he was being promoted to General a few days before leading a fly-by at President Eisenhower's funeral in 1969. Soon afterward, General Yeager became the Vice-Commander of the 17th Air Force. In early 1971, Brigadier General Yeager arrived in Pakistan as the U.S. Defense Representative to Pakistan. His job was to teach Pakistanis how to use American military equipment.

Chuck was the first and youngest military pilot inducted into the Aviation Hall of Fame in Dayton, Ohio (1973). He took his last military flight in 1975 in an F-4 Phantom II—one of his favorite planes. He retired from the Air Force in 1975, although he continued to fly for the Air Force and NASA as a consulting test pilot. President Gerald Ford

Chuck logged more than 10,000 hours flying in military and experimental aircraft over his career.

Chuck may have retired from the military, but he sure hasn't retired from flying.

presented him with the peacetime version of the Congressional Medal of Honor in 1976.

Over his career, Chuck Yeager flew over 180 different military aircraft and logged more than 10,000 hours. There were five planes named for Glennis. In 2004, Chuck Yeager is still jetting across the country making speeches and appearing at aviation events and shows.

The Experimental Aircraft Association (EAA) presented him with their Freedom of Flight Award (1994). In 1995, he took over the association's Young Eagles Program as Chairman.

Celebrating the 50th anniversary of his historic flight in the X-1, Chuck flew a new F-15 Eagle, named appropriately Glamorous Glennis. At the end of the flight, General Yeager told the crowd, "The Air Force taught me everything I needed to know and gave me a tremendous education. What I am . . . I owe it all to the Air Force."[1]

FYInfo
For Your Information

The Young Eagles

A Young Eagle

The Experimental Aircraft Association's Young Eagles Program began in 1992. Cliff Robertson, the first Chairman, and Tom Poberezny, the EAA's President at the time, flew the first Young Eagles during the EAA's Fly-In Convention in Oshkosh, Wisconsin. The convention is an annual event. The Young Eagles Program offers free flights to children between 8 and 17. All a child has to do is show up on a day when the Young Eagles are providing flights. These special days are sponsored year round at airports all across the country.

EAA members wanted to expose more young people to aviation. One way to do that was to take as many children on flights as possible. That's how the Young Eagles Program was born. The original goal was to fly 1 million Young Eagles by the one-hundredth anniversary of the Wright brothers' first powered flight on December 17, 2003. In November 2003, the program reached that goal.

Currently, over 36,000 EAA members participate in the program. Pilots volunteer their time, fuel, and their aircraft to expose children to the thrill of flying. Other members volunteer their time and services in other ways. They make phone calls, schedule flights, and so on. During the time that Chuck Yeager was Chairman of the group, he flew over 200 Young Eagles.

If you want to learn more about aviation, you might consider the EAA Academy's Resident Summer Youth Camp. Certified flight instructions run this program for boys and girls age 12 to 18. Kids learn more about aviation and get to share their love of aviation with other like-minded kids.

Chronology

1923 Chuck Yeager was born on February 13 in Myra, West Virginia

1929 Stock market crashes on October 29

1941 Enlisted in Army Air Corps as a private; Pearl Harbor attacked by Japan on December 7, pulling United States into World War II

1942 Entered the Flying Sergeants Program to train as a fighter pilot; met his future wife, Glennis Dickhouse

1943 Received pilot wings

1944 Flying P-51 Mustang in combat over England; shot down over occupied France and made his way back to England; became first ace-in-a-day on October 12; first pilot to shoot down a German jet (Me262)

1945 Maintenance Officer for Lockheed P-80 Shooting Star, America's first jet fighter

1947 Was the first person to fly faster than the speed of sound in the Bell X-1; awarded Mackay Trophy and Robert J. Collier Trophy from the National Aeronautic Association; awarded the FAI Gold Medal by the International Aeronautical Foundation

1948 Air Force announces 1 Mach flight to public; received honorary degree from West Virginia University

1949 Flew X-1 in first runway takeoff on January 5

1952 Graduated from Air Command and Staff School

1953 Broke the flight speed record by flying Mach 2 in the Bell X-1A; elected one of the Ten Outstanding Young Men by the Junior Chamber of Commerce

1954 Took command of the 417th Fighter Squadron

1961 Graduated from Air War College

1962 Began the first Commandant of the Aerospace Research Pilot School

1963 Was nearly killed testing the NF-104 rocket aircraft—first to eject in a full pressure suit used for high altitude flights

1966 Took command of the 405th Fighter Wing and flew 127 missions in Vietnam

1969 Became Vice-Commander of the 17th Air Force and was promoted to Brigadier General; received honorary degree from Marshall University

1973 Inducted into the Aviation Hall of Fame

1975 Retired from active duty

1976 Awarded the peacetime Congressional Medal of Honor

1981 Inducted into the International Space Hall of Fame

1985 Awarded the Presidential Medal of Freedom; awarded the Theodore Roosevelt Distinguished Service Medal by the Theodore Roosevelt Association; awarded the Bradford Washburn Award by the Boston Museum of Science; Kanawha Airport in West Virginia is renamed Yeager Airport

1986 Sits on presidential commission to investigate the Space Shuttle Challenger disaster

1994 Awarded EAA's Freedom of Flight Award

1995 Became Chairman of EAA's Young Eagles Program

1997 Made his last flight as a military consultant on the 50th anniversary of his history-making flight in the X-1

2005 According to several sources, a movie about the legendary Chuck Yeager is in the works at 20th Century Fox

Timeline in History

1784	Edward Warren is the first airborne American, taking a flight in a balloon in Baltimore, Maryland
1903	The Wright brothers take their first flight at Kitty Hawk
1908	Henry Ford introduces the Model-T; first motion pictures taken during a flight; first passenger flight; first military pilots to fly in service; first airport, Morris Park in New York City, is established; the first passenger fatality in a powered airplane
1910	Glen Curtiss is the first to receive a pilot's license; Orville Wright opens the first commercial flight school in Montgomery, Alabama; first mile-high flight; first women, Blanche Scott and Medlar Raiche, fly solo just days apart; Theodore Roosevelt, although out of office, is the first President to fly; first flight from a battleship, the USS *Birmingham*
1911	Harriet Quimby is the first woman to receive a pilot's license; first aircraft lands on a ship, the USS *Pennsylvania*; first transcontinental flight from New York to California of 49 days and 69 stops ends
1912	Parachutes were invented
1914	World War I begins; first scheduled airliner flight: St. Petersburg to Tampa, Florida
1919	First transatlantic flight
1921	First pressurized cabin; German battleship *Ostfriesland* is sunk by bombs dropped from Army aircraft; first air-to-air refueling when Wesley May stepped from the wing of one biplane onto the wing of a second biplane with a five-gallon can of gasoline strapped to his back
1923	First nonstop transatlantic flight
1925	First scheduled air freight service, implemented by auto manufacturer Henry Ford
1926	Army Air Corps is established
1927	Charles Lindbergh is the first to fly solo across the Atlantic Ocean
1929	Robert Byrd flies over the South Pole
1931	Auguste Piccard is the first to reach the stratosphere during flight; Wiley Post completes his first flight around the world in 8 days and 16 hours with navigator Harold Gatty
1932	Amelia Earhardt is the first woman to fly solo across the Atlantic Ocean
1933	Wiley Post completes his solo flight around the world in 7 days and 19 hours
1934	Goodrich Corp builds the first pressurized flight suit for high altitude flying
1939	The first commercial flight across the Atlantic Ocean; first successful single main rotor helicopter flight; Germans fly the first turbojet airplane
1947	Chuck Yeager is the first person to break the sound barrier during flight
1949	First nonstop flight around the world
1953	Chuck Yeager is the first to fly twice the speed of sound
1957	Jackie Cochran is the first woman to fly supersonic
1958	NASA is founded
1961	The Soviet Union wins the first leg of the space race, launching the first man into outer space
1962	The X-15 experimental rocket research plane penetrates outer space
1969	Neil Armstrong, a United States astronaut, is the first man to walk on the moon
1983	Sally Ride is the first United States woman astronaut to enter outer space
1986	The U.S.S.R. launches the space station, *Mir*; the space shuttle *Challenger* explodes just seconds after launching; *Voyager* is the first craft to fly around the world without refueling
1990	The Hubble telescope is launched into space
1997	The United States probe, *Pathfinder*, begins transmitting images of Mars back to earth
2004	Two United States robots begin their journey on Mars; first private aircraft to reach space
2005	Steve Fossett became the first to fly solo, nonstop around the world in a 66 hour flight

Chapter Notes

Chapter 2 A Country Boy

1. General Chuck Yeager and Leo Janos, *Yeager* (Bantam, 1985), p. 12.

Chapter 3 Behind Enemy Lines and Back Again

1. General Chuck Yeager and Leo Janos, *Yeager* (Bantam, 1985), p. 28.
2. Ibid., p. 46.

Chapter 4 Breaking the Sound Barrier

1. General Chuck Yeager and Leo Janos, *Yeager* (Bantam, 1985), p. 127.
2. Ibid., p. 130.
3. Ibid., p. 134.

Chapter 5 The End is Just the Beginning

1. Edwards Air Force Base, Public Affairs, "Aviation Legends' Trialogue Recalls Past Days of Flying, Fighting, Fishing" (November, 2002), http://www.edwards.af.mil/archive/2002/2002-archive-trialogue_recalls.html

Medals and Awards

Military Service:

Air Force Commendation Medal
Air Force Outstanding Unit Award
Air Medal
Bronze Star
Distinguished Flying Cross
Distinguished Service Medal
Legion of Merit
Purple Heart
Silver Star
Special Congressional Silver Medal

Non-military:

Bradford Washburn Award
Congressional Medal of Honor
Federation Aeronautique International Gold Medal
Golden Plate Award
Harmon International Trophy
Honorary degrees from West Virginia University and Marshall University
Horatio Alger Award
Inducted into Aviation Hall of Fame
MacKay Trophy
Presidential Medal of Freedom
Robert J. Collier Trophy
Theodore Roosevelt Distinguished Service Medal

Glossary

Aerodynamic (ae-roh-di-NAM-ik)
Designed with specially rounded edges to reduce wind drag.

Buzz (BUHZ)
A fast flight close to the ground.

Cryogenic (kri-uh-JEN-ik)
Related to extremely low temperatures.

Evadee (ee-VA-dee)
Trooper that makes it back from behind enemy lines.

Flak (FLAK)
Bullets from huge ground guns. These guns shoot many bullets in fast succession.

Flying ace (FLI-ing AC)
Today, the term refers to a pilot who has shot down five (or more) enemy aircraft. The term flying ace was first used to describe Adolphe Pegoud. He was a French pilot and the first pilot to shoot down five German aircraft in World War I.

Fuselage (FUZH-uh-lagh)
The main body part of an aircraft to which the wings and tail are attached.

Jettison (JAET-a-san)
To force the fuel tanks to drop all the fuel, usually in the air where the fuel evaporates.

Mach (MAHCK)
The term used to measure supersonic speeds.

Sonic boom (SAH-nik BOOM)
A sonic boom is the noise you hear from a shock wave. Supersonic flights produce a sonic boom. They're very loud and sound like an explosion. The shock wave is strong enough to break windows if the aircraft is low enough to the ground.

Subsonic (SUHB-sah-nik)
Flight speed below the speed of sound.

Supersonic (SOOP-r-sah-nik)
Flight speed at the speed of sound and beyond.

Transonic (TRAN-sah-nik)
Flight speed range from just below to just above the speed of sound.

For Further Reading

For Young Adults

Ayres, Carter M. *Chuck Yeager: Fighter Pilot*. Lerner, 1988.

Cox, Donald W. *America's Explorers of Space*. Hammond, 1967.

Leerhsen, Charles. *Press on! Further Adventures in the Good Life*. Bantam, 1988.

Wolfe, Tom. *The Right Stuff.* Bantam Books, 1980.

Works Consulted

Holmes, Tony (Ed), and Scutts, Jerry. *Osprey Aircraft of the Aces, 1: Mustang Aces of the Eighth Air Force.* Osprey Publishing, 1994.

Levinson, Nancy S. *Chuck Yeager: The Man Who Broke the Sound Barrier*. Walker & Co., 1988.

Lundgren, William R. *Across the High Frontier: The Story of a Test Pilot, Major Charles E. Yeager, USAF*. Morrow, 1955.

Spick, Mike. *Milestones of Manned Flight.* Smithmark Publishers Inc., 1994.

Yeager, General Chuck, and Janos, Leo. *Yeager*. Bantam, 1985.

Yenne, Bill. *Legends of Flight with the National Aviation Hall of Fame.* Publications International, Ltd., 1997.

On The Internet

Aerospaceweb.org
http://www.aerospaceweb.org

Chuck Yeager's Official Web Site
http://www.chuckyeager.com

Chuck Yeager.org
http://www.chuckyeager.org

Edwards Air Force Base/About Edwards (Gallery)
http://www.edwards.af.mil/about_edwards/index.html

Glenn Research Center, Speed of Sound
http://www.grc.nasa.gov/WWW/K-12/airplane/sound.html

NASA
http://www.hq.nasa.gov/office/pao/History/X1/chuck.html

Yeager Open House Display 2000
http://www.cebudanderson.com/yeagerdisplay09.htm

Young Eagles
http://www.youngeagles.org/default.asp

Index